D0007122

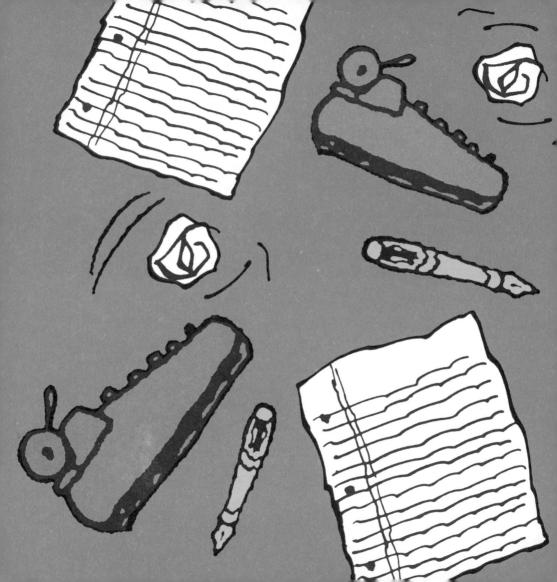

The Literary Ace Strikes Again!

by
SCHULZ

HarperCollins*Publishers*

So, You Want To Be A Writer?

YOU SHOULD WRITE A SELF-HELP BOOK..

YOU KNOW, TO HELP THOSE WHO ARE LONELY AND CAN'T GO ANYPLACE..

How to be Happy Even Though You're Stuck in the Back Yard.

So, You Want To Be A Writer?

Everyone's
A Critic

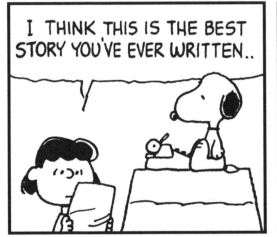

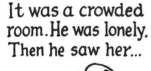

Publish
Or
Perish!

Publish Or Perish!

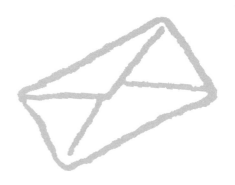

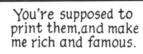

Dear Editor,
Why do you keep sending my stories back?

You're supposed to print them, and make me rich and famous.

What is it with you?

Gentlemen,
   Regarding the recent rejection slip you sent me.

I think there might have been a misunderstanding.

What I really wanted was for you to publish my story, and send me fifty thousand dollars.

Didn't you realize that?

If we sell it, we'll print another.

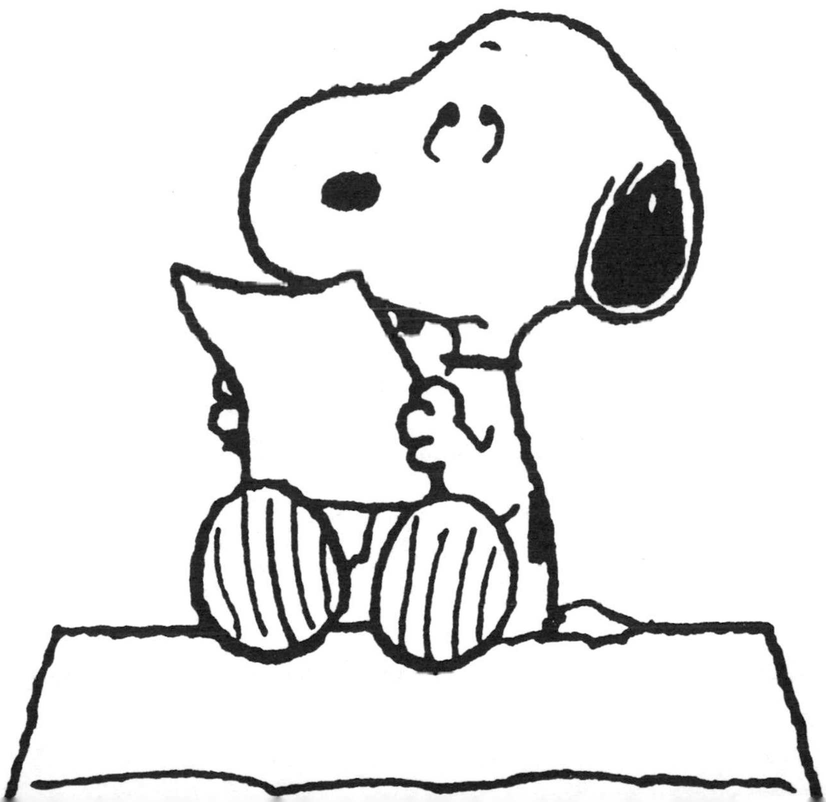

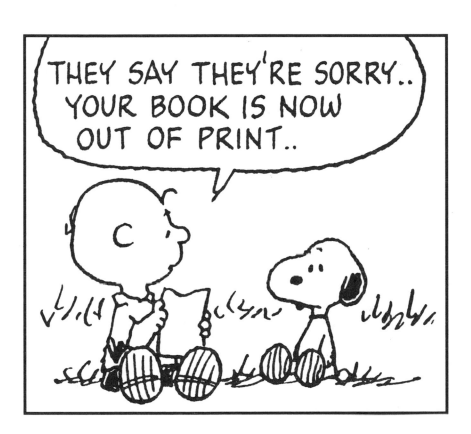

Like all great writers, I have known suffering.

≡ HarperCollins*Publishers*

Produced by Jennifer Barry Design, Sausalito, CA
Creative consultation by 360°, NYC.
First published in 1997 by HarperCollins*Publishers* Inc.
http://www.harpercollins.com

ISBN 0-06-757448-3

Printed in Hong Kong

1 3 5 7 9 10 8 6 4 2

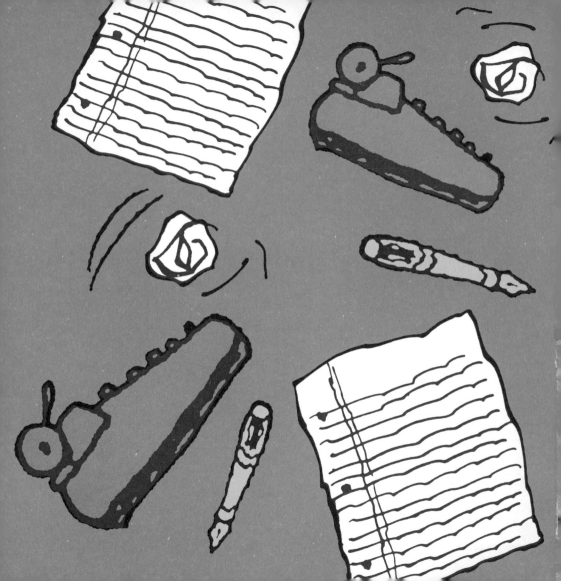